Abandoned Farmhouse

Abandoned Farmhouse
and other haiku

Second Edition

Edward J. Rielly

PRESS HERE

Press Here
22230 NE 28th Place
Sammamish, Washington
98074-6408 USA

ISBN 978-1-878798-41-1

Copyright © 2021 by Edward J. Rielly

All rights, including electronic rights, reserved. No part of this book may be reproduced or transmitted by any means without the written permission of the author and/or publisher, except for brief passages quoted in reviews or scholarly articles.

The author gratefully acknowledges the editors of the following publications in which some of these poems appeared in present or previous versions: *Acorn*, *A Hundred Gourds*, *Akitsu Quarterly*, *Autumn Moon*, *Bottle Rockets*, *Brussels Sprout*, *Cattails*, *Dragonfly*, *Frogpond*, *Haiku Headlines*, *Haiku Quarterly* (U.S.), *Haiku Zasshi Zō*, *Heron's Nest*, *Hummingbird*, *Kō*, *Mayfly*, *Modern Haiku*, *New Cicada*, *New England Letters*, *Paper Wasp*, *Potpourri*, *Shemom*, *Timepieces 1995* (Cloverleaf Books, 1995), and *When Butterflies Come: 1993 Haiku Society of America Members' Anthology* (Haiku Society of America, 1993).

Design and typography by Michael Dylan Welch.
Headings in 18/20 and 14/17 Cooper Std Black.
Poems set in 12/20 Adobe Garamond Pro.

For my children, Brendan and Brigid, who remember.

And for the next generation
that did not know the farmhouse:
Morgan, Shannon, Maura, Sadie, and Molly.

~ Introduction

I grew up on a farm in southwestern Wisconsin between Darlington and Mineral Point, a dairy farm that my father operated with my mother, brothers, and sister. Many of the following haiku arose from that heritage—reflecting, I think, both the beauty and sadness of farm life. I prize my years on the farm. They have contributed more than I can measure to who I am and therefore to my writing.

A time came, however, when no one was left to milk the cows and mend the fences. My father died, and later my mother followed. I was off in Maine teaching and directing the writing and publishing program at Saint Joseph's College in Standish, although I have recently retired. My remaining brother—the first two having also passed away—was not able to handle the farm. So he, my sister, and I decided to do what needed to be done—sell the farm.

By that time, the farmhouse had stood empty for several years, my mother having moved to town for her final years. Legally, neither the farm nor the farmhouse was abandoned; we owned the farm and kept the buildings from falling into complete decay, although emptiness tends to weather buildings more quickly than does living in them. Psychologically, though, it seemed as if we had abandoned the farmhouse, leaving it spiritually empty, almost like letting a dear friend or relative live in loneliness, deteriorating slowly without the comfort of others to share intimately in the person's passing.

The following "Abandoned Farmhouse" haiku reflect my years on the farm. The other haiku, arranged seasonally, are more diverse in content, but many of them also come out of my Wisconsin farming background.

Readers, I trust, will not see the farmhouse haiku as unrelentingly sad. There remained too much of our love in that house. Even today, when another family owns and lives in the farmhouse, there remains joy in the memories of how we lived within its walls through days of cranked telephones and rural party lines, through each season of welcoming new calves and lambs, baling hay, picking corn, and breaking ice out of the stock tank so the cows could drink. Had writing these haiku not been at heart a joyous experience, even a celebration, I think that I would have left them unwritten.

More than two decades have passed since this book's first edition appeared. I have retained the poems that I originally included, sometimes with slight changes, and added new haiku to both sections of the book. A welcome aspect of the past is that it does not recede for me but instead journeys along as I move into the future, the way the moon seems to travel with you when you take a night drive. The new haiku reflect this journey—mine and my past.

Edward J. Rielly
Westbrook, Maine

Abandoned Farmhouse

abandoned farmhouse:
    in the roadside mailbox
        an empty bird nest

abandoned farmhouse:
    blackened clothespins
        on a sagging line

abandoned farmhouse:
    my autograph
        in cracked concrete

abandoned farmhouse:

    how cool the air

        beyond the cellar door

abandoned farmhouse:
    something scratching
        inside the furnace

abandoned farmhouse:
    wallpaper peeling back
        to my childhood

abandoned farmhouse:
    the quiet bedroom where
        I waited for morning

abandoned farmhouse:
    cricket sounds filling the room
        where father slept

abandoned farmhouse:
    a yellowed grocery list
        taped to the countertop

abandoned farmhouse:

    a moth flies out

        of the water faucet

abandoned farmhouse:
    my daughter snaps a picture
        of the sagging front porch

abandoned farmhouse:
    the nearby climbing tree
        now a stump

abandoned farmhouse:
    linoleum patch indented still
        where the freezer stood

abandoned farmhouse:

    stairway to our bedrooms

        creaking just a bit more

abandoned farmhouse:

    touching the stovepipe

        that warmed my pajamas

abandoned farmhouse:
    a faded newspaper that lined
        the pantry shelf

abandoned farmhouse:
    snatches of silent conversation
        in the once-busy kitchen

❧ Other Haiku

Spring ❧ **Ray of Light**

spring wind:
a leftover leaf lands
on my windshield

in the middle
of a puddle remembering
the hole in my shoe

spring cleaning
a shoe box full
of old poems

climate change . . .
my old globe
gathering dust

eye surgery—
learning to see all things
a little differently

blue sky sliced
by a cherry tree branch;
clouds of blossoms

ray of light—
dust motes break
against my hand

brown caterpillar
crossing the parking lot . . .
Sunday mass just out

spring morning
even in the rain
a robin

cactus transplant
my fingers still feeling
its spines

spring rain
the priest hurries
through his homily

small town flood
everyone turns out
to see the governor

washing dishes . . .
an ant on the sink
scurries away

planting season
the crate of mail-order hostas
on my porch

Summer ~ **A Violet Blooming**

    her hand
    on mine—
    fireflies

    small fan
    cooling the spot
    where we made love

freshly washed counter—
lethargic ant studying
the new ant bait

summer sunset . . .
rain in a broken bottle
turning to wine

dark night
looking again for fireflies
to light my way

tornado funnel;
the child's pinwheel
faster and faster

girl's fingers
on the boy's shoulder . . .
rose petals falling

sunshine returns—
in the trees still
the sound of rain

in a dried hoof print
on the cow path
a violet blooming

stacking bales
on the hay rack—
my sense of place

summer vacation:
the fragrance
of the lilac bush

rumble of thunder . . .
scent of lilacs fills up
the waiting for rain

Fall ↢ **One Brown Leaf**

amid sunflowers
a rooster's red comb
rises and falls

young girl's face
red in the wind:
last apples on the tree

the moon
eyeing me
without a blink

aquarium
boy grinning
at the shark's teeth

autumn dusk
deflated football
on a closet shelf

touchdown pass
a stranger insists
on a high-five

autumn fly
turning itself upside down
on my mirror

this life—
shaking dust off my shoes
at the front door

one brown leaf
in the middle of the maple;
her first cancer pains

red apple dropping
into the fire
of the sun

garbage truck—
our jack-o'-lantern's smile
drooping

early morning walk:
under the white moon
a twig snaps

Winter ～ **Snow Gathering**

snowfall
the silence we share
side by side

silence
before the snowstorm
deepening

inch by inch
snow gathering
on our porch steps

old dog falling
by the ice-covered fire hydrant—
the look in his eyes

January wind:
an old farmer hides his face
from the auctioneer

early morning highway . . .
out of the dark countryside
a house full of light

the fire engine's
quiet departure . . .
silent cattle

winter rain
nothing seems quite
to be itself

under the snowbank
sound of water seeping
into the sewer

end-of-season storm—
snowblowing a new path
from me to you

seventieth birthday:
the icicle outside my door
begins to melt

ꙮ About the Author

Edward J. Rielly is a professor emeritus of English and former director of the writing and publishing program at Saint Joseph's College in Standish, Maine. A widely published author, his books include a memoir of his childhood (*Bread Pudding and Other Memories: A Boyhood on the Farm*), children's picture books, biographies, cultural histories, studies of baseball and football, and many collections of poetry. His haiku have appeared in several chapbooks and dozens of magazines since the 1970s. His *Answers Instead: A Life in Haiku* is the 2016 recipient of the Kanterman Memorial Award from the Haiku Society of America. He lives in Westbrook, Maine, with his wife, Jeanne.

❧ Other Books by the Author

Haiku

Answers Instead: A Life in Haiku, Encircle Publications, 2015
Abandoned Farmhouse and Other Haiku, Press Here, 2000
    (first edition)
Anniversary Haiku, Brooks Books, 1997
The Furrow's Edge, chapbook; Juniper, 1987
Family Portrait, Advance, 1987 (chapbook)
Rain Falling Quietly, Wind Chimes, 1985 (chapbook)

Tanka

A Bed of Geraniums, Encircle Publications, 2019
How Sky Holds the Sun, AHA Poetry, 1998 (online)

Other Poetry (some including haiku or tanka)

Beautiful Lightning: Spiritual Poems in a Difficult World,
    Resource Publications, 2019
Some Things Still the Same, privately printed, 2018
To Sadie at 18 Months and Other Poems, Moon Pie Press, 2011
Old Whitman Loved Baseball and Other Baseball Poems,
    Moon Pie Press, 2007
Ways of Looking: Poems of the Farm, Moon Pie Press, 2005
A Fine, Safe Journey, Pudding House, 2003
My Struggling Soil, Plowman Press, 1994
The Breaking of Glass Horses and Other Poems, Great Elm, 1988

Memoir

Bread Pudding and Other Memories: A Boyhood on the Farm,
    Little Creek Press, 2014

Children's Picture Books

Jugo Meets a Poet, Shanti Arts Publishing, 2015
Spring Rain/Winter Snow: Seasonal Haiku,
 Shanti Arts Publishing, 2014

Other Books

*The Sister Fidelma Mysteries: Essays on the Historical Novels
 of Peter Tremayne*, McFarland & Company, 2012
Legends of American Indian Resistance, ABC-CLIO, 2011
Murder 101: Essays on Teaching Detective Fiction,
 McFarland & Company, 2009
Football: An Encyclopedia of Popular Culture,
 University of Nebraska Press, 2009
Sitting Bull: A Biography, Greenwood Press, 2007
*Baseball in the Classroom: Essays on Teaching the National
 Pastime*, McFarland & Company, 2006
F. Scott Fitzgerald: A Biography, Greenwood Press, 2005
Baseball: An Encyclopedia of Popular Culture,
 University of Nebraska Press, 2005
Baseball and American Culture: Across the Diamond,
 Haworth Press, 2003
The 1960s, Greenwood Press, 2003
Baseball: An Encyclopedia of Popular Culture, ABC-CLIO, 2000
Approaches to Teaching Swift's Gulliver's Travels, MLA, 1988

www.ingramcontent.com/pod-product-compliance
Lightning Source LLC
Chambersburg PA
CBHW022341040426
42449CB00006B/663